Conversations with the Holy Spirit

MORE THAN A FRIEND

30-DAY DEVOTIONAL FOR KIDS

By Sheba

Scan to listen to the Fruit of the Spirit

More Than A Friend Devotional
© 2025 Sheba
All rights reserved.
No part of this publication may be reproduced, stored in a retrieval system, or transmitted in any form or by any means—electronic, mechanical, photocopying, recording, or otherwise—without the prior written permission of the author, except for brief quotations used in reviews, articles, or scholarly works.
Scripture quotations are taken from various translations of the Bible. Unless otherwise noted, all Scripture quotations are taken from the Holy Bible, New International Version® (NIV®). Copyright © 1973, 1978, 1984, 2011 by Biblica, Inc.™ Used by permission. All rights reserved worldwide.
Additional quotations may be taken from the New Living Translation (NLT), copyright © 1996, 2004, 2015 by Tyndale House Foundation. Used by permission of Tyndale House Publishers, Carol Stream, Illinois 60188. All rights reserved.
Other versions are indicated where used.
ISBN:979-8-9877179-3-6
Published by Sheba Empowers
Printed in the United States of America

Acknowledgment

I want to thank my "Elizabeth," Ashley Lunnon. When this vision leaped, we brought it to life together. Thank you for giving me that final push I needed to cross the finish line.

My Leading Lady, Apostle Ann Marie Alman, you've taught me 'game changer' writing strategies. For that, I want to say thank you!

#GodfortheWIN

Dear Parents and Caregivers,

Thank you for opening this devotional and for your commitment to nurturing your child's faith. This book supports your vital role, offering clear, practical ways to engage your child in daily faith conversations and growth.

With many distractions, finding time to connect with your child and God is more important than ever.

The following pages offer simple and meaningful opportunities for easy faith conversations. Even brief, imperfect moments matter. You don't need perfection; just making time counts.

Here are a few ways to get the most out of this book:

- Choose a time that suits your routine, such as breakfast, bedtime, or while on the go. Consistency matters most. If starting out, try one brief session a week to build the habit.

- Ask questions. After reading, use discussion prompts to encourage your child to share their thoughts and ideas. There are no wrong answers; this is a safe space to explore faith. Adjust prompts for your child's age and understanding.

- Embrace conversation. The devotional is a starting point. Let stories and verses inspire deeper talks about God's truths in your child's life.

- Pray together. Use the provided prayers as guides, but encourage your child to pray in their own words. Personal prayer is powerful for children.

Witnessing your child's faith journey is a beautiful adventure. Challenging days are normal. Perseverance strengthens your bond and your child's faith. Thank you for your time and love. We pray that this book blesses your family and helps you grow closer to one another and to God.

With gratitude,

Sheba

15 GUIDING QUESTIONS FOR DEEPER THOUGHT & ENGAGEMENT:

Choose one or two questions to guide your conversation each day

What did you learn today?

What does today's reading teach you about the Holy Spirit?

Is there something that you want to do differently after reading this today?

Did anyone/anything come to mind after reading this?

Why should this be important to us?

Was there something that you did not understand about what you read?

Do you know what _____ means?/Tell me what you think _____ means.

How could we apply what we read today?

Would you like to share something that happened to you that reminds you of this?

How do you feel after reading this today?

When do you feel that you need the Holy Spirit most?

When we read this, do you need help from the Holy Spirit in this situation?

How do you want the Holy Spirit to help you today?

When you prayed today, how did you feel?

What did you enjoy the most about what you read?

Day 1

Bullying and cyberbullying

> Hebrews 12:14 "Make every effort to live in peace with everyone"

Bullying is the total opposite of what this scripture encourages, whether you bully others or you are being bullied. God called us to love our neighbors, not to make fun of them, threaten them, or cause any harm—emotionally, physically, or mentally. When someone is bullied, it causes a lot of hurt, and the person doing the bullying is also hurt. While bullying happens for many different reasons, we should never find joy in hurting others.

Prayer: Dear Holy Spirit, please protect me today. Empower me with courage to be strong and kind to others, no matter who they are and what they look like. Help those who bully to understand that their words and actions can hurt others. Help me to remember that you will always protect me. Amen

Day 2

Peer Pressure/Compromise

> 1 Corinthians 15:33 "Do not be deceived: Bad company ruins good morals"

Our true self is revealed when we are under pressure or when others are not watching. Your response to peer pressure can help you understand who you truly are, and it can also serve as a guide, helping you identify areas in your life where you need to improve. Just remember: Every decision has an outcome. The outcome may be immediate or delayed, but there always is one. The great news is that you get to choose based on your decisions.

Prayer: Dear Holy Spirit, I want to do what is right, even if no one is watching. Guide me to be in the right place, at the right time, and to always do what is right in Your sight. I want to achieve only positive outcomes from my decisions. Amen

Day 3

Conflict with family/friends

> Proverbs 15:1 "A gentle answer turns away wrath, but a harsh word stirs up anger"

Everyone faces conflict, even with those closest to us. When challenges arise, try viewing them as opportunities to learn something new about yourself or the other person, since every problem has multiple solutions. By being mindful of what we say and how we say it in a heated moment, we can avoid unnecessary trouble.

Prayer: Dear Holy Spirit, words can hurt, but they can also heal. In moments of conflict, help me stay calm and show love and respect to my loved ones. Amen

Day 4

Loneliness

> Hebrews 13:5 "I will never leave you; never will I forsake you"

Sometimes, when we feel alone, it is the enemy deceiving us with a lie. The truth is that we can never be alone; God would not allow it. He surrounds us with people who love and care for us, and we also have Him. I can admit that He is the best company ever!

Prayer: Dear Holy Spirit, I feel lonely. Let me feel your presence every day. I will not believe the enemy's lies. Let me remember that you will never leave me alone, because you care for me. Amen

Day 5

Difficulty making new friends

> Proverbs 18:24 "A man who has friends must himself be friendly, but there is a friend who sticks closer than a brother"

Friendship is a huge part of growing up; some friends come, and some go. It can be a challenge to make new friends, but the great part is that God is always ready to help. When you are friendly, it is only a matter of time before you make good ones, at that!

Prayer: Dear Holy Spirit, forming good friendships is important to me, and I find it challenging at times. May I always be friendly, and may the friends you send into my life be kind, compassionate, understanding, and fun! Amen

Day 6

Maintaining friendships

> Proverbs 27:17 "As iron sharpens iron, so one person sharpens another"

What joy it is to have friends! The Bible says that a true friend is always loyal (Proverbs 17:17). Loyalty in friendship means being there for someone even when times are tough, standing by them through their ups and downs. For young people, this can mean supporting a friend when they are stressed about upcoming exams by offering to study together or checking in with a friend who is having family issues to let them know they aren't alone. It looks like keeping promises and supporting someone even when it's inconvenient. When loyalty is present, even in the face of challenges, the friendship will endure.

Prayer: Dear Holy Spirit, I just want to thank you for my friends. Give me the strength to be there for others, showing compassion and love. Amen

Day 7

Loss/Grief

> **Psalm 34:18 "God is close to the brokenhearted"**

Losing someone or even something is hard; the grief we may feel could be unbearable. God wants to come close to those who experience these emotions to comfort them. No one should grieve alone.

Prayer: Dear Holy Spirit, my heart is hurting. I find it hard to process; all I am left with are memories. Help me cherish those memories and appreciate the people in my life. Amen

Day 8

Poor communication skills

> **Ephesians 4:29 "Do not let any unwholesome talk come out of your mouths, but only what is helpful for building others up, as it fits the occasion, that it may give grace to those who hear."**

No one says the right things all the time; we are human, and we make mistakes. However, this scripture makes it pretty clear how we should speak, always to build up and not to tear down. To help communicate more effectively, consider a few practical tips: pause and think before speaking, choose words that affirm others, and actively listen to understand. If, for any reason, we do not communicate properly, the best way to make things better is to offer an apology.

Prayer: Dear Holy Spirit, whenever my words are harsh, help me to be gentler. Teach me how to speak the truth in love. Open my eyes to see how my words affect others. Amen

Day 9

Confusion

> James 1:5 "If any of you lacks wisdom, let him ask God, who gives generously to all without reproach, and it will be given him"

Life in itself can be confusing. Everyone loses their sense of direction from time to time. Do not beat yourself up. God gives the greatest directions.

Prayer: Dear Holy Spirit, sometimes I feel lost and confused, yet I know you are with me, guiding me on the right path. Please show me and teach me everything I need to know. Amen

Day 10

Anger

> James 1:19 "My dear brothers and sisters, take note of this: Everyone should be quick to listen, slow to speak, and slow to become angry"

The truth about anger is that we all experience anger in response to certain things. Whenever you feel yourself getting angry, count down from 10 to 1 or take a few deep breaths. Remember, just as we trust God's plan and let the Holy Spirit guide us in our lives, we can seek that same comfort when anger arises. When you are calm, those feelings may change, and you can listen more effectively with a heart open to God's wisdom. Listen before you speak!

Prayer: Dear Holy Spirit, help me to stay calm when I am upset. Bring peace to my heart, mind, and soul. I want to always think before I speak. Amen

Day 11

Jealousy/Comparison

> Galatians 5:26 "Let us not become conceited, provoking and envying each other"

Jealousy is more common than some people would like to admit. Did you know that God said that He is a jealous God? You just want to be sure that it remains a feeling; do not let it settle into your heart and mind. Feelings change, accept it, be honest about it, and share your feelings with someone you love and trust. No one will be upset about how you feel; they will understand, even God.

Prayer: Dear Holy Spirit, help me not to compare myself to others. Let me be grateful for what I have and for the people in my life. I want to celebrate with others and believe in you for what I want and need. Amen

Day 12

Dishonesty

> Proverbs 12:22 "Lord detests lying lips, but he delights in people who are trustworthy"

People often lie because they see no other option. Sometimes, it's from fear of discipline or correction. Children and adults both need correction. It helps us grow! Don't be afraid. Honesty is always the best policy.

Prayer: Dear Holy Spirit, I lie at times, and I am sorry. Give me the courage to be honest, even if I am corrected. Help me trust that You will be with me and guide me as I grow. Amen

Day 13

Sickness

> Jeremiah 30:17 "For I will restore health to you, and your wounds I will heal"

God does not like it when we are sick, so He promised to help us get better. When you are sick, always ask God to heal you. Soon, you will feel like yourself again. Don't forget to eat your fruits and vegetables, too!

Prayer: Dear Holy Spirit, please remove all germs and sickness from my body, not just now but even in the future. Thank you for healing me. Amen

Day 14

Lack of empathy

> **Romans 12:15** "Rejoice with those who rejoice, and weep with those who weep"

Life is hard. We often focus on our own needs and wants, becoming self-centered and overlooking the needs of others. To love our neighbors, put yourself in their shoes. If they're facing a bad day or a challenge, consider what would help you feel better and aim to offer that support. Strive to be that kind of person.

Prayer: Holy Spirit, open my heart to others. Show me when selfishness creeps in. Fill me with Your generosity and compassion, so I can truly love my neighbor as You love me. Amen

Day 15

People pleasing/Lack of boundaries

> Galatians 1:10 "Don't try to please people, but please God"

The primary message is to prioritize pleasing God above all else, as it is impossible to please everyone. Follow His word and obey Him.

Prayer: Holy Spirit, I know I can't please everyone. Empower me to seek to please God always. Amen

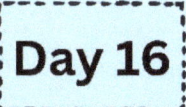

Social anxiety/Anxiety/Fear:

> Psalm 56:3 "When I am afraid,
> I put my trust in you"

Fear is one of the earliest emotions we feel. Fear of the dark, bugs, loud sounds, heights, the Dentist, needles, and many others. God does not want fear to overwhelm us; He wants us to have courage, knowing that He is with us and it is His job to ensure our protection. When you feel afraid, take a deep breath and try to calm your mind. Talk to a trusted adult about your feelings and pray for the courage to do so. God is good at protecting us!

Prayer: Dear Holy Spirit, let me have courage every day. If I am afraid, remind me that You are bigger and braver than anything I am afraid of. Amen

In your own words, talk to God about your fears. Share honestly what worries you and open your heart to Him. He is always there to listen and help you through any challenge.

Day 17

Low self-esteem

> Psalm 139:13-14 "For You formed my inward parts; You covered me in my mother's womb. I will praise You, for I am fearfully and wonderfully made"

Inspired by this scripture, look in the mirror and name what you love about yourself. Saying phrases like "I am beautiful" or "I am smart" are affirmations. Focus more on your strengths than your flaws. God loves you and created you in His image.

To help, you can pray: 'Dear Holy Spirit, I sometimes struggle with my appearance.' I wish I were taller, smarter, or had a different nose, but I want to accept myself for who I am. Thank you for loving me as I am. Amen

Day 18

Impulse behavior/Lack of self-control

> Galatians 5:22 "But the Holy Spirit produces this kind of fruit in our lives: love, joy, peace, patience, kindness, goodness, faithfulness, gentleness, and self-control"

After considering how the Holy Spirit helps us grow in self-control, let's think about everyday challenges. Candy, ice cream, and soda are treats many of us enjoy, but sometimes we have too much. The Holy Spirit is present to guide us. Enjoying snacks in moderation is a gentle step toward good health.

Prayer: Dear Holy Spirit, thank you for all the foods I enjoy. Teach me self-control so that I do not overeat and live a long, healthy life. Amen

Day 19

Pride

> Proverbs 16:18 "Pride goes before destruction, and a haughty spirit before a fall"

Building on this scripture, here is a life lesson to remember: You are no better than anyone, and no one else is better than you. This will help keep you far away from pride; Pride destroys everything!

In response, let us pray: Dear Holy Spirit, when I feel prideful, may I remember to humble myself. Let me be more like Jesus. Amen

Day 20

Emotional dysregulation

> **Colossians 3:12** "Therefore, as God's chosen people, holy and dearly loved, clothe yourselves with compassion, kindness, humility, gentleness and patience"

It is essential to be gentle and patient with others, but do not forget to extend the same kindness to yourself. Perhaps you are experiencing challenges. Stay calm and remember that you can depend on God to make things better.

In prayer, you can seek this gentleness and patience: Dear Holy Spirit, when I face challenges, help me remain calm and guided by your peace. Strengthen me so that my emotions do not overcome the grace you give. May your presence fill me with lasting peace and resilience. Amen

Day 21

Increased social withdrawal/Isolation:

> Matthew 11:28 "Come to me, all you who are weary and burdened, and I will give you rest.

When we notice ourselves withdrawing or avoiding friends, it may seem natural to isolate, but doing the opposite—reaching out—can lighten our mood and help us feel better, as the Scripture invites us to seek rest.

Following this, let us pray: Dear Holy Spirit, when I feel alone and overwhelmed with sadness, show me your love, remove whatever causes me distress, and comfort me. Amen

Day 22

Family conflict or instability

> Psalm 46:1 "God is our refuge and strength, an ever-present help in trouble"

Arguments happen. People who love one another have disagreements. However, it is important not to let issues linger. As we reflect on Psalm 46:1, let us remember that God has blessed us with our family, forgiveness, love, and beautiful memories.

Prayer: Dear Holy Spirit, keep my family together. When we have fights, Holy Spirit, bring peace. Help us to forgive, guide us as we create new memories, and let love always unite us. Amen

Day 23

Feeling misunderstood

> Jeremiah 12:3 "But as for me, Lord, you know my heart. You see me and test my thoughts..."

When you feel misunderstood by others, remember that God knows you deeply. He understands your heart and thoughts. He created you for a reason, so even when people cannot see your true self, rest assured that God does.

Prayer: Dear Holy Spirit, help me remember that God knows me best. Guide my words and actions. Amen

Day 24

Excessive screen time/Addiction

> **1 Corinthians 10:13** "No temptation has overtaken you except what is common to mankind. And God is faithful; He will not let you be tempted beyond what you can bear"

Can you imagine what your day would be like without a phone, tablet, or television? Our devices can be used for learning, but just like too much ice cream, they can cause harm. Your eyes, mind, and body are affected by what you watch and listen to. Enjoy your shows, have fun, but also make time every day for activities that don't involve your screens. Challenge yourself to set aside a specific time each day to engage in screen-free activities, such as playing sports, learning a musical instrument, or spending quality time with friends and family. These activities not only keep you active but also help you build stronger relationships and skills. Take the first step today and choose one fun screen-free activity!

Prayer: Dear Holy Spirit, never let me love anything more than you. Help me spend more time away from screens and devices, as excessive use can have a negative impact on me. I struggle with [specific struggle, e.g., checking my phone too often, or needing it to fall asleep], and I seek your guidance to overcome this challenge. Encourage me to grow closer to you and find joy in moments without screens. Amen

Day 25

Difficult life events/Transitions

> Proverbs 3:5-6 "Trust in the LORD with all your heart and lean not on your own understanding; in all your ways submit to him, and he will make your paths straight"

Just as the morning always comes after the night, challenges in life do not last forever. It is natural to feel sad or worried during difficult times. Allow yourself to feel these emotions, and remember that God and the people in your life, such as a parent or caregiver, care for you deeply. Reach out to them for support—they want to help you. You can always ask them to pray with you, and they will be glad to do so!

Prayer: Dear Holy Spirit, what I am facing seems overwhelming. Please help me to trust you more each day. Give me the strength to get through these hard times and fill me with joy and happiness again. Amen

Remember, you can talk to God just as you would to a friend. Tell Him what is in your heart, in your own words. Whether it is a big worry or a small one, He is listening. Prayer is a personal conversation, and you don't need to use special words or phrases to engage in it. Just be yourself and speak from the heart.

Day 26

Moving to a new school or community

> **Psalm 121: 8** "The Lord will watch over your coming and going, both now and forevermore"

Being in a new school or community can come with its challenges, but it can also be an exciting time to make new friends and create more memories. New things can be a blessing!

*Prayer: Dear Holy Spirit, change is hard. I will admit that, but keep me open to new things and let me see the blessing in being in a new school or community.
Amen*

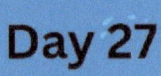

Academic Challenges

> Philippians 4:13 "I can do all things through Christ who strengthens me"

School is where you will spend most of your day. Everyone is good at something, and if math or science is hard for you, that is okay. Be proud of what you do well and ask for help in areas where you need it. Join various activities or clubs and consider what you truly enjoy doing. This will help you find out what you are good at and what you enjoy. You might be surprised by how much you can learn. Recommendation: Say the scripture each morning before school.

Prayer: Dear Holy Spirit, give me the mind of Christ and strengthen me in school to do my absolute best. Help me focus on my studies, calm my nerves when I feel overwhelmed, and encourage perseverance through challenging times. With your help, I am confident that I can overcome every challenge and achieve great things. Amen

Day 28

Rejection

> Psalm 27:10 "Though my father and mother forsake me, the Lord will receive me"

It doesn't feel good to be rejected, because God wants us to enjoy our family and friends and live a good life. God accepts you; you do not have to do anything for Him to love you or to stop loving you. His love is unconditional.

Prayer: Dear Holy Spirit, thank you for loving and accepting me. When I feel left out, help me remember this, and let your love fill my heart with hope and strength. Amen

Day 29

Greed/Selfishness

> Luke 12:15 "A man's life is not measured by the many things he owns"

You may wonder why your parents tell you to share with others, whether it's a sibling, cousin, friend, or neighbor. Sharing is important because it helps us avoid selfishness. Just as God showed generosity by giving us Jesus, His one and only Son, we learn the value of sharing through His example.

Prayer: Holy Spirit, you give to me; help me give to others. Make me generous. Amen

Day 30

Identity conflicts

> Ephesians 2:10 "For we are God's handiwork, created in Christ Jesus to do good works, which God prepared in advance for us to do"

God had a purpose in mind when He created you: you are His handiwork, created in Christ Jesus to do good works. If you are unsure of who you are and what your unique purpose is, turn to scripture for guidance. Remember, you were created for good works because God loves you deeply. Reflect on the significance of being chosen and loved by the Creator of the universe. To better understand God's purpose for you, take daily steps—pray for clarity, seek service opportunities that reveal your strengths, and engage with mentors or faith community members who can support your journey.

Prayer: Dear Holy Spirit, show me who I am in Christ and prepare me for good works. Help me to dedicate time to personal reflection, through prayer or journaling, so that I may deepen my spiritual understanding and connection with You. Strengthen me to step forward with faith, knowing You have set a meaningful purpose for my life. Amen

About the Author

"Sheba" is a leader in Early Childhood Education and a passionate advocate for women's empowerment. She serves as a Professional Development Specialist with the Council for Professional Recognition, Adjunct Lecturer at CUNY School of Professional Studies, and Career Advisor for the NY Early Childhood Professional Development Institute.

As Founder of Sheba Consults LLC and Den Leader of SHEBA Women's Empowerment Group ("She's Better After it ALL"), she coaches women to rise with bold truth, grace, and purpose. Known for her engaging "Sheba-style" delivery, she has spoken at podcasts, forums, and international platforms.

Her creative works include Heart of Gold, Just Like God,, The Bed I Choose, and the children's worship album Songs for Jesus: A Child's Heart. Beyond writing and speaking, Sheba leads charitable initiatives in the U.S. and Nigeria, where she also launched the "Dear Men" clothing line promoting anti-domestic violence.
A proud mother of four, Sheba continues to build a legacy of faith, education, and empowerment.

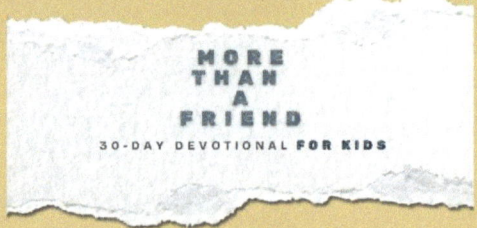

Have you ever wondered how faith can help you be your best whenever you need it?

Do you want to know how to handle everyday situations or face challenges like a champion?
Imagine reducing school stress or making friends without anxiety.

This devotional offers guidance and comfort—especially when school work feels challenging or
when understanding your friends matters most.

The Holy Spirit is real—not an imaginary friend—even though He is always with you. This devotional helps kids get to know and talk to the Holy Spirit on a daily basis. Parents can read along with their children, discuss the messages, or pray as a family.

With short, easy-to-understand devotions and inspiring prayers, this book helps you build a lifelong friendship with God's helper, offering guidance and peace.

Start your conversation today!

www.ingramcontent.com/pod-product-compliance
Lightning Source LLC
Chambersburg PA
CBHW041404090426
42743CB00006B/150